My goal is to

Entertain ■ Educate ■ Empower

children by telling meaningful Stories
while teaching Sign Language!

Mr.C

Best Day Ever!
Birthday Surprise Story
ASL - American Sign Language Book for Kids and Beginners
Stories and Signs with Mr.C - Book 6

Story Written by Mr.C - Randall Clarkson

Design & Illustrations by Deonna Clarkson

© 2016 by RDCmedia—Randall & Deonna Clarkson

StoriesAndSigns.com

Positive Repetition

is a learning method that rewards your child in a positive way.

- **Read through the story in one sitting**. Note that the words printed in color correspond with the characters in the pictures above.

- **Go back to the beginning of the book and begin to sign**. Your child will see the signs as an actual part of the story which is now familiar to them.

- **Parents can sign the two signs** shown on each page and have your child copy you. Try not to touch their hands as they first struggle to find the sign themselves. They are exploring how they can manipulate on their own.

- **Note the <u>underlined words</u>**. These are the sign language words which were read and signed earlier in the story.

- **Continue to re-read each book** until all the signs listed in the back are learned. Your child will love re-reading the books and the feeling of mastering the signs more and more.

- **Use these new sign language words** throughout the day, reinforcing them to memory.

The **Positive Repetition** of the sign language words will

engage the memory, entertain the heart **& empower your child**.

Thank you for giving your child the gift of Sign Language!

Best Day Ever!

BOOK 6 of the Stories and Signs Series

by

Mr.C

Randall Clarkson

*"At the end of this book,
I have two special gifts just for you!
Be sure and use your hands to
learn the sign words!"*

Mr.C

(tele) phone

Stick out your thumb and
pinkie finger - put your thumb
on your ear

yes

Make an "S" fist
Shake it back & forward like
nodding your head

Austin was sitting in his kitchen when the telephone started ringing.

"Hello..." There was a long quiet pause as someone spoke to his Mom but he couldn't tell what they were saying.

Mom answered,
"Yes...No...No...Yes...
No...Yes...OK!" and she hung up.

"Who was on the phone Mom?" Austin asked.

talk

Put your pointer finger on your lips - make a downward circle with your finger

play

Make two fists with pinkies and thumbs sticking out - turn hands toward you and then away from you

"That was Logan's Mom," his Mom said.

"What did she talk about?" he asked.

"She talked about the weather and then she asked if you wanted to come over and play with Logan today" she said.

Austin decided to rap his answer. "She called on the Phone, Phone, Phone... now I want to Play, Play, Play...oh yah!"

friend

Lock your two pointer fingers
together - turn your fingers
over and lock them again

jump

Pointer and middle finger act
like legs and jump up and
down on the other hand

Logan was Austin's best friend and they're about the same age.

"Oh! Can I? Can I? Can I?" he said while jumping up and down, "Can I go play with my best-best-best friend?"

"Well, O..."

[BAMM] went the front door before his Mom could even finish saying O.K.!

Who is *your* best friend?

run - ran

Hook pointer finger to thumb of other hand - hop them forward

door

Make two "B" hands side by side with palms outward - right hand turns in like a door

Austin was running down the sidewalk and down the street to Logan's house. He ran up the front steps onto Logan's porch and pounded on his door.

[BAMM! BAMM! BAMM!]

[Ding Dong! Ding Dong!]

The door opened up and Logan's Mom said with a smile, "Who is making all that noise!? Oh, it's you...come on in."

hug

Cross your arms and HUG your heart

game

Make two fists with thumbs sticking out - bump together pinkie fingers

"Logan!!" "Austin!!" they yelled as they gave each other a tackle football hug.

"Come on, Austin, let's play some games in my room!" said Logan.

So they did.

They played every game Logan had and then they made up some of their own.

Do *you* like to play games?

Which ones?

soup

Make a bowl hand - curve
pointer + middle fingers of
other hand - scoop from
hand to mouth

rest

Cross your arms and lay your
open hands on chest

Just when their stomachs started to rumble. **[GrrrBlub]** Logan's Mom made them sandwiches and bowls of soup. Yum!

Once they slurped their soup and chewed their sandwiches it was time to take a rest. They told each other that they wouldn't sleep, but they were both...so...tired...

[Zzzz-Zzzz]

When they woke up from their rest, something had changed!

pirate

Put cupped hand over one
eye and growl "Arrr"

shovel (dig)

Pretend you're holding a
shovel - start digging with it

They had become Pirates!!!

"Arrr, Logan should we go out the <u>door</u> and look for 'barrried' treasure in your back 'yarrrd'?" Austin said in his best pirate voice.

"Arrr Austin. Let's dig with shovels!" said Logan.

They found two shovels and a bucket to put their treasures in.

Can *you* <u>talk</u> like a pirate? Try!

dirt

Both hands palms up - rub fingers together like you're feeling the dirt

dig (shovel)

Pretend you're holding a shovel - start digging with it

In Logan's back yard they <u>ran</u> to their favorite dirt pile and started digging while they made up <u>pirate</u> songs. They dug up treasures (worms, bugs, and slugs) and put them into their treasure chest (bucket).

After the treasure chest was full of wiggling "treasures," these good <u>pirates</u> put the extra dirt back into the hole so that none of their <u>friends</u> would fall in and get hurt.

home

Bunched fingers and thumb - touch the chin and then touch the upper jaw

hole

Make an "O" hand - draw a circle with pointer finger of other hand

"Arrr Logan. Let's go put the treasure over 'yonderrr'," Austin said, still _talking_ like a _pirate_.

"Arrr Austin. Let's give this treasure a new home," replied Logan.

So they _dug_ a new hole in the _dirt_ on the other side of Logan's yard and dumped the treasure in the hole and covered it up.

Do _you_ like to _dig_ in the _dirt_ with a _shovel_ like a _pirate?_

ship - boat

Cup your hands together
Move them forward in little
spirts like a boat on waves

tree

One arm is horizontal
Other hand makes a tall "5"
Wiggle fingers like branches

"Arrr Logan, shall we climb into the <u>pirate</u> ship?" Austin said as he pointed up to Logan's tree <u>house</u>.

"Shiver me timbers...I think that's a good idea!" yelled Logan as he <u>ran</u> for the tree.

They <u>talked</u> like <u>pirates</u> as much as they could and then laughed as they tried to make up stories about what they saw from their <u>pirate</u> ship.

"Ahoy mate...Shiver me timbers!"

time

Point to wrist of other hand where a watch would be

sad

Open hand starts at your eyes and drops down past your chin - look sad

They heard the <u>telephone</u> ringing and Logan's Mom saying, "<u>Yes</u>...No...<u>Yes</u>...OK!"

"That was Austin's Mom. It's time for Austin to go <u>home</u> now," Logan's Mom said.

"Does he *have* to? We're having so much fun!" said both boys with sad faces.

"Yes, it's time for ye <u>pirates</u> to be gittin' <u>home</u>!" boomed Mom, using *her* best <u>pirate</u> voice.

fun

Put out first two fingers of
each hand - one set of fingers
taps your nose then taps the
top of the other two fingers

smile

Two pointer fingers draw a
smile on your face starting on
your chin upward

It's not easy to quit <u>playing</u> when you're having fun. But Logan remembered one of his Mom's rules.

If I don't obey...I can't <u>play</u>!

"O.K. goodbye Logan. I'll see you later," said Austin as he <u>jumped</u> down from the <u>tree</u>.

"Bye Austin", said Logan as he smiled and giggled.

Why do *you* think Logan is smiling and giggling as Austin is leaving?

alligator

Lace hands together in front of you - open and close hands up and down

walk

Both hands flat with palms down - take a couple steps

"See you later alligator," Austin said as he went out the door and down the sidewalk back to his house.

He took his time walking home and studied some ants that were walking across the sidewalk. Hmm...why do they walk in a line?

As Austin slowly climbed up his front porch, he thought that he heard something. Curiously, he opened the front door.

surprise

Both hands pinched together
beside eyes - quickly move
them up into open hands

laugh

Two pointer fingers point to
each end of mouth and
wiggle fingers

"Surprise!"

Right there, in Austin's <u>house</u> were all of his family and all of his <u>friends</u>...including Logan!

"I knew about your party but I couldn't tell you about the surprise!" said Logan.

Austin <u>smiled</u> and laughed as everyone started singing...

happy

Open hands palms to chest -
brush your shirt upward
two times

birthday

Touch your chin with your
middle finger then touch
chest with same middle finger

Happy Birthday to you,

Happy Birthday to you,

Happy Birthday dear Austin,

Happy Birthday to you!

funny

Pointer and tall finger brush
against nose and down

candle

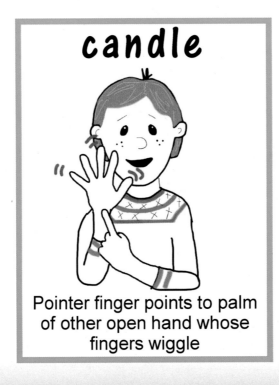

Pointer finger points to palm
of other open hand whose
fingers wiggle

They played <u>games</u> and <u>laughed</u> as they all told funny stories about each other!

Before Austin blew out the candles on his <u>birthday</u> cake he stopped and closed his eyes.

"I wish..." and then he whispered the rest so no one could hear.

Do *you* make a wish on your <u>birthday</u> before blowing out *your* candles?

thank you

Flat open hand (fingertips against chin) and then let it fall forward

O.K.

Make an "O" hand

Make a "K" hand

Austin used really good manners. After he opened each present, he said thank you to the person who gave it to him. He even remembered to read the cards too!

He still hadn't opened the gift that he had wished for...but that's OK. Now that he's a year older he knows we don't always get what we wish for.

We should be thankful for what we get, right?!

big

Put open hands together in front of you - pull them apart quickly

box

Pretend to touch both sides and front/back of a square box

There was just one more present… and it was big! The <u>funny</u> card was from his Mom and Dad.

After he took off the bow and wrapping paper, he opened the big box and saw…nothing!

The box was empty! He sat and thought about it for a while and finally told his parents, "<u>Thank you</u> for the big box! I can put lots of <u>games</u> into this big box and it will help to keep my room clean!"

parents

Open palm hand - touch thumb to chin and up to forehead

open

**Both hands up, palms out
Thumbs together
Push up and out to open**

He <u>ran</u> over and gave them a <u>big</u> <u>hug</u>!

Austin's parents <u>smiled</u> and told him what a nice <u>thank you</u> he'd given them.

They then <u>laughed</u> and said that he should go see what is on the front porch!

He took off <u>running</u> and opened the front <u>door</u>. There...on the porch...was *exactly* what he had wished for!

bicycle

Both fists move in circle away
from body like bike pedals

wow

Two "W" hands on each side
of mouth - make an "O" with
open mouth

A brand new bicycle!!!

It was red, shiny and just his size. It had a horn and shiny fenders.

"WOW!" Austin kept saying over and over, "WOW!"

By the <u>time</u> everyone had gone <u>home</u>, it was dark so he couldn't ride his new bike. Austin would have to wait until morning.

Do *you* have a bicycle? If so, what color is it?

sleep

Start fingers at forehead - pull them down into a first as you close your eyes

best

Open hand across mouth - pull quickly to the side into a fist with thumb up

Logan got to stay for a sleep over. They talked and talked about how fun the day had been.

The boys laughed about surprising Austin for his birthday.

"It's time to quiet down and get to sleep," whispered Austin's Dad.

"Thanks Dad...this was the best day ever!"

Austin went to sleep with a smile on his face and his shiny, red bicycle right next to his bed!

More **Stories and Signs** with Mr.C

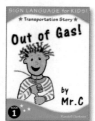

★ **The ABC's** — ASL Alphabet Signs

#1 **Out of Gas!** — Transportation Story

#2 **No Animals in the House** — Animals Story

#3 **The Big Sandwich** — Fun Foods Story

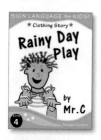

#4 **Rainy Day Play** — Indoor & Outdoor Play

#5 **Molly's Puppies** — Days of the Week

#6 **Best Day Ever!** — Birthday Surprise

#7 **Company is Coming!** — Cleaning My Room

#8 **Haunted Baseball Park** — Being Brave & Smart

Can you Sign these words from the Story?

(wow)

- telephone
- yes
- talk
- play
- friend
- jump
- run
- door
- hug
- game
- soup
- rest
- pirate
- shovel
- dirt
- dig—dug
- home
- hole
- ship
- tree
- time
- sad
- fun
- smile
- alligator
- walk
- surprise
- laugh
- happy
- birthday
- funny
- candle
- thank you
- O.K.
- big
- box
- parents
- open
- bicycle
- wow
- sleep
- best

The more I practice, the better I become! - Mr.C

We would like to dedicate this book to
our five amazing Grandchildren...

Meadow ♥ Logan ♥ Dani ♥ Austin ♥ Drew

...and the thousands of kids who
have learned sign language words
while laughing & enjoying our stories.

Mr.C   AUTHOR/TEACHER/PAPA
Mrs.C   ILLUSTRATOR/GRAMA

Made in the USA
Monee, IL
26 August 2022